CARNATIONS

ELEGANCE IN FLORAL ARRANGEMENTS

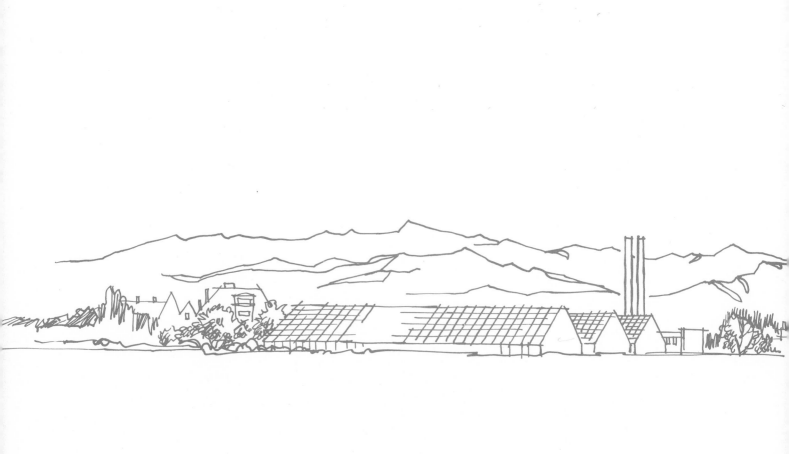

CARNATIONS

ELEGANCE IN FLORAL ARRANGEMENTS

COLORADO FLOWER GROWERS ASSOCIATION, INC.

DENVER, COLORADO

This book is dedicated to all the growers
of flowers everywhere in the world.

*"Flowers and fruits are always fit presents: flowers,
because they are a proud assertion that a ray of beauty outvalues
all the utilities of the world."*

Ralph Waldo Emerson
Essay on "Gifts"

Library of Congress catalog card number: 68-9279

Published by

COLORADO FLOWER GROWERS ASSOCIATION, INC.

909 SHERMAN STREET
DENVER, COLORADO 80203

Printing and Binding by Egmont H. Petersen Co. Copenhagen, Denmark

Contents

Acknowledgements

Each endeavor survives and succeeds because of the belief of the author in what he is doing. How well, however, this creative endeavor is fostered by equally steadfast belief coming from friends and supporters! It is a pleasure to express my heartfelt thanks to my associates and close friends both in and out of the carnation growing business for their warm encouragement on the entire project.

At a professional level, I would be remiss if I failed to acknowledge a deep personal obligation to the following people:

Mr. Robert Gries of San Francisco –– a peerless commercial photographer who nurtured an amateur interest in photography in me to the full-fledged desire to do my professional best;

Mr. Reuben Botshon –– friend, *confidante,* fearless critic of anything that has been done, and tireless advisor on the production of this book;

Grace Breathwaite –– stylist for the book's many accessories and ever constant worker and supporter of the project in its darkest as well as its lightest hours.

Every photographic book has enormous problems in acquiring the use of the kind of properties which are most appropriate for a given area or occasion. Since the purpose of this book is to encourage people to use their own personal treasures in creating a setting for flower arrangements, we have frequently "put upon" our friends to loan us the accessories which they have acquired over the years. These friends, all from the Denver, Colorado area are: Mrs. Norman G. Christensen, Mrs. Dorothy Conroy, Mrs. Keith Davis, Mrs. Mel Davis, Mrs. B. G. Hammans, Mr. Homer Hill, Mrs. Laura Kintzele, Mrs. James K. Meyer, Mrs. Clara Nickerson, Mrs. Reba Paludan, Mrs. Helen Crabbs Rippey, Mrs. Sam G. Russell, Mrs. Arthur Vos, Mr. Mather C. Wallis, Mrs. Robert C. Whitney, Mrs. John Zimmermann, also Autrey Brothers Incorporated, Colorado College, Fuji En Restaurant

Out gratitude also to TWA for their loan of a model of the air transport of tomorrow.

Finally, no single person has all of the *objets d'art* that are required for a book of this size. To fill these gaps, we are most grateful to our friends at Denver Dry Goods Company, Howard Lorton Galleries, May D & F, and Neusteters, four great stores in the United States who have given us free access to the abundance of wonderful items which they offer for sale every day to their customer group.

⸮ Foreword ⸜

THE CARNATION ... the Greeks had a name for it ... The Divine Flower ... *Dianthus Carophyllus* ... if you use the Latin form ... translated to mean Flower of Zeus (or God to the ancient Romans) ... with the scent of clove.

Elegance in a vase, on a lapel, as a gift, or a miracle of God's creation as you hold it in your hand. Fragile, yet sturdy. Delicate, yet long-lived. Subtly colored. Long-stemmed. Queenly, graceful, fragrant.

These are the words which flood through the mind as one contemplates the natural beauty of a carnation.

This lovely flower is the inspiration for our book. There has never been a major book in color on carnations, or the variety and visual intrigue which they offer to the flower arranger. May you enjoy our treatise on "The Divine Flower" and find inspiration in the floral designs which have been produced for you.

History of Carnations

There are many varieties of carnations in the world. All carnations belong to that family of flowers known as "Pinks". The *genus* or family name is *Dianthus*. These blooms occur in nature in everything from tiny, single flowers to the large multi-petalled blossoms you get from your florist. Some members of the family, commonly grown as a garden flower, are produced from seed.

Where seeds are used, the resulting blooms occur in a wide variety of variegated colors and solid shades from white through yellow, orange, pink, red, lavender and purple. Carnation flowers grow true to the color and type of flower on the end of a specific stem, however, only when they are reproduced from slips or cuttings from the same stem.

Historical records of carnations extend all the way from modern times back into antiquity. They grew as wild flowers on the hillsides of ancient Greece 3,000 years before the birth of Christ. They are recorded in pre-Christian writings in the days of the full glory of the Roman Empire, in drawings and writings from Elizabethan times, in the art and literature of the Renaissance, and in other historical records that have come to us from the past. Early kings, noblemen, and merchants sat for their portraits sometimes holding a carnation, or next to a bouquet of them placed on a table.

Shakespeare wrote about carnations in "A Winter's Tale," when he has Perdita say, "The fairest flowers o' the season are our Carnations." This was in the year 1601, and from that date on, the name "Carnation" appears to have been attached to the plant.

During the 18th century a popular social activity was the "tailoring" of carnations – the individual trimming of each petal with a razor or very sharp knife to produce a flower of perfect form. In the seventeen and eighteen hundreds, the carnation blossom was used as a spicing or

flavoring addition to hot, mulled wines, wherein the wine picked up the clove-like aroma and flavor of the carnation blossom which was soaked in it.

Carnations are an important foundation for the perfume industry in France. In the warm, sunny fields of southern France, in Grasse, a village close to Monaco, for years huge fields of carnations have been grown for use as a basic essence in quality perfume.

Today, where carnations or "Pinks" are grown in household gardens, they are generally of the type which are usually started from seed. Flowers tend to be small and numerous along the stems which radiate from the plant, and the color is widely varied. These carnations are always colorful, and their fragrance is entrancing.

The large, single carnation blooms which are typical of the flowers sold by your florist are grown from cuttings. Each plant is disease-free, and its flowers have been produced in a sterile environment which results in improved flower size, better color, and better keeping quality.

The carnation is the most widely grown commercial cut flower in the world. It represents about twenty-five percent of all the cut flowers used in flower shops. Except for the miniature carnations (where a number of flowers are produced on each stem), carnations used by florists have a single, large bloom at the top of a sturdy, straight stem.

Over forty individual hand operations are needed to bring each flower from cutting to mature blossom. Flower stems are disbudded to remove side blooms so that all of the vigor of the plant goes to the flower at the end of the stem. Each stem is kept straight through the use of individual string and wire stalls. Every plant is watered, fed, warmed in winter and air-conditioned in summer, provided with extra carbon dioxide to promote the development of plant food, fogged to prevent development of fungus growths, and fumigated to eliminate insect pests.

Each *Dianthus Carophyllus* you get from your florist is a tribute to hard work, years of experience, and an ultimate scientific achievement as a disease-free plant selected and bred to produce a flower of maximum vitality, color, and perfection in beauty and form.

About the Author

What would induce Harry A. Lazier, a technical and advertising writer, to produce and illustrate a book on flower arrangement? We find the beginnings of an answer to this question in the following statement:

"If there were two things that distinguished Harry in his boyhood, I would say the first was a boundless enthusiasm and energy for doing and trying everything that the world had to offer. Second, he always felt that anything was susceptible of being learned by anybody. Consequently, there was no field however technical, nor any endeavor however complex, into which he was unwilling to poke an inquisitive finger."
So said the author's mother, when asked to recall what would qualify her son to write a book about flower arranging.

True to what his mother has said, Harry Lazier not only wrote this book, but also did all of the flower arrangements himself, lighted them and took their pictures with an 8 × 10 view camera. His pleasure in flower arranging as a personal hobby, which later evolved into an important phase of his multifaceted career, has made him an enthusiastic missionary for the idea that anybody who tries flower arranging will have a good time.

Born and raised in Dixon, Illinois, Harry received his B.S. degree from Northwestern University. After graduation he moved to Denver, where, after a few years in the advertising department of a large manufacturing concern, he joined the advertising firm of Henderson, Bucknum and Company, of which he is now part owner and a senior partner.

In his professional life he has been a creative writer of advertising and publicity, a motion picture and still photographer, and account supervisor on many varied advertising accounts.

In recent years, Harry has become one of the nation's experts in the field of flower promotion and commercial floral marketing, and in the process, an accomplished public speaker.

As a friend and business associate for many years, I have found that Harry Lazier's impact in the profession of his choice –– in the community where he has worked, lived, and raised his family –– and on his many friends across the nation –– is that of a vital creative being, with a gift of humor and energy which leaves you breathless, but better for the experience.

James S. Holme

Flower Arranging as an Art

Flower arrangements are an art form. They fall into an art category which is like a "stabile." Every arrangement is three-dimensional, and although it grows (because cut flowers are alive until they "go to sleep") for practical purposes, it doesn't move. Its shape and form and size vary as one moves around it and observes it from different sides. If it is well done, it will be pleasing to look at from almost any angle.

Some flower arrangements are not made to be viewed from a 360-degree perspective. These arrangements are generally finished on the front and both sides, but not on the back, and are intended to be placed up against a wall or in a corner where movement of the viewer around the arrangement is limited by the walls of the room.

As an art form, flower arranging has many variables – the color of the flowers themselves, difference in size of the flowers, foliage differences, variables in container and, finally, variations in the shape or form of the arrangement itself.

Like all art forms, flower arranging skill improves with practice. The beginning flower arranger will be lacking substantially in skill in the first arrangement he or she makes. Skill will grow with practice and with experience in handling flowers and foliage and putting them together into pleasing designs. Like all art experience, the production of a flower arrangement is an intensely personal endeavor. Its satisfactions in terms of artistic expression are equally individual and personal. Unfortunately, a large body of material on flower arranging has sprung up and put into print which tends to limit the effort of flower arrangers through establishment of rigid rules and regulations aimed at helping both the beginner and the old hand. The restrictions on self-expression imposed by these rules may frequently have a severely inhibiting effect on a beginner, who feels unable to qualify as a flower arranger in good standing unless he is acquainted with and adheres to all of the thoughts which have been put forth on what constitutes a pleasing or well-done arrangement.

Because floral design is self-expression in an art form, it is essential that the floral artist give full reign to his creative instinct and impulse. There can be no inhibitions in approaching the problem of producing a pleasing arrangement. To achieve this happy goal, we need to substitute one simple rule for all the rules in the book. That rule is, "If the flower arrangement you create is aesthetically pleasing to you, it has served an artistic and worthwhile purpose."

This rule is really no rule at all. Rather, it is a premise which anybody who wants to try to arrange flowers can accept. It stimulates interest in sitting down for the first time and tackling the job of using flowers to make something pretty. As the flower arranger pursues his hobby, his skills will grow. The things he does today may not be the same as the things which please him tomorrow, but this is always a mark of personal growth in an artistic endeavor. Following this precept, even the most timid person would be willing to attempt at least one flower arrangement. There can be no fear of failure, because the absence of rules for performance guarantees that there are no standards which might serve as a measurement of failure.

Thus, our simple flower arranging philosophy provides the basis for happy pursuit of an art form and a hobby which will be satisfying as long as flowers grow and as long as people are around to arrange them in bouquets.

Let's state our principle once again,

"If the flower arrangement you create is aesthetically pleasing to you, it has served an artistic and worthwhile purpose."

As we mentioned in the Foreword, our book deals with flower arranging, using carnations exclusively with a variety of different foliages and properties. We have chosen the carnation as the floral foundation for our arrangements in the interest of maintaining simplicity of design and theme in every flower arrangement which is illustrated.

The carnation is an ideal flower for our purpose, because of the variety and color, size of blossoms, and variegations which occur. In addition to the variety available through color and flower size, variance in containers and in foliage adds extra creative dimensions to the arrangements you will see.

Most flower arrangement books show broad selections of flowers. We have limited our book to only one flower – the carnation – because of its beauty, as well as our belief that the mixture of a wide variety of flowers with different shapes, textures and colors defeats the simplicity of purpose which prompted this work.

The Chinese philosopher, Ching Ch'ien-te, said, "Only one or two kinds of flowers should be arranged in a vase. If too many kinds are used together, they are unappealing." We claim no credit for originating something new in doing a book exclusively on one flower. We are happy that the flower we have chosen for our book is so versatile that it provides a

fine opportunity for flower arrangers.
In this book, you are going to see every
style, shape and color of flower arrangement imaginable. You are going to see
these arrangements put into every
conceivable situation. You will behold
arrangements placed in settings of total
elegance and complete humility. Every
kind of property from sterling silver to
leaves which have fallen from the trees
will be placed in juxtaposition with the
arrangements – every color you can think
of will be used – every conceivable form
and style.

Inevitably, these arrangements will seem
to fall into some sort of pattern, because
the mechanical job of putting them
together results in patterns. These patterns
are geometric. They take the shape of
lines, circles, triangles and curves and
right angles. They also include other
geometrical shapes besides the flowers, in
the form of pictures, utensils, patterns, and
even the lights and shadows which become
part of the total composition when the
flower arrangement has been placed in its
final setting.

No flower arrangement is an
absolute. Nor does it represent inviolable
rules for putting together flowers and
accessories. Once again, we return to the
only rule we followed in executing every
one of the bouquets in this book – "If the
flower arrangement created is aesthetically
pleasing to the creator, it has served an
artistic and worthwhile purpose."

You will note in our book a short
description of how each arrangement is

put together so that you can understand
how the mechanical problems of producing
each one are solved. You will not be able
to reproduce each example exactly no
matter how hard you try, because every
flower in the world grows in its own
particular way with crooks in its stem and
leaves curled in patterns as individual as
your own fingerprints. You may
approximate these pictures, but you can
never duplicate them exactly. Nor, if you
believe in our philosophy, would you
want to.

Today YOU are the floral artist. YOU
are the master of the artistic experience
on which you are about to embark.

YOU are the creator.

We sincerely believe that what YOU
are going to do is aesthetically worthwhile,
because YOU like it.

CARNATIONS

ELEGANCE IN FLORAL ARRANGEMENTS

Design Delight

Beginnings are usually elemental. One object.
One happening. One result. And so it is with this beginning.
One carnation in a simple vase . . .
one sprig of green . . . one Swedish doily.
And yet, how lovely is the result of this beginning!
You only need a small container, one flower, and a bit of foliage.
Think of twelve flowers. A few containers. For a few dollars,
you can bedeck your dwelling with the ultimate grace ——
fresh flowers in every corner.

Single flowers in bud vases

are logically followed by more complicated forms.

So, advancing from a single carnation in a bud vase,

here are three carnations in a simple silver cream pitcher.

The foliage is spiral eucalyptus.

A china cream pitcher would do equally well.

Or any small container ... on a tray ...

a small napkin ... or a place mat.

A simple arrangement but beautiful,

with all of the elegance of a much more elaborate design.

Wouldn't you like to try it?

Fill the cream pitcher with saturated floral foam. The first flower is cut to a length approximately three times the length of the pitcher and put in place.

The lowest flower is placed next, close to, but not obscuring, the pitcher handle, as it is important to preserve the shape and identity of the container.

The third and final flower is placed on the opposite side of the lowest carnation and halfway between the top and bottom flowers for balance.

Spiral eucalyptus fills in the open space and covers floral foam. This easiest of floral arrangements achieves its elegance through simplicity of form and design.

To proceed up the ladder of learning

about flower arranging, let us consider what could be done

with five carnations that would be different.

Here is one answer —— a vertical, linear arrangement in a cylindrical black vase

that is strikingly different.

It can be arranged using either a pin frog or floral foam to hold the flowers.

Wouldn't this bouquet by an "eye stopper"

for any corner in your home?

Simple as this arrangement looks, there are two tricks that simplify its construction. First trick —— place the tallest flower first and then the bottom carnation.

Next, place the middle flower. This establishes the stem lengths for the last two flowers. If you worked from the top down, this would be a problem.

Place the last two carnations. Trick number two —— tie the carnation stems so that they stay together with several pieces of fine wire, string, or thread.

The ties create the linear effect. Now, soften it with three sprigs of huckleberry. Unfinished in the back, the flowers must be placed against a wall.

This cone-shaped swirl of carnations requires very precise placement of each flower. Start with the tallest two at the back of the arrangement.

*T*hink differently!

Think big! Let your imagination go! And grow.

Think of a brand new way to arrange carnations —

seven flowers in a conical swirl with a teakwood

heron in the middle.

Think swirls, circles, ellipses, triangles, ovals.

Every arrangement shape is lovely when

it is expressed in carnations.

Place the next two flowers to continue the descending pattern. Stem length and angle of placement are critical in maintaining the conical shape.

Finish the conical swirl pattern with the bottom three flowers coming down and around the bowl to cover the front lip of the bowl.

Design Delight ... pages 22 and 23

Add a spear-like foliage of some type in radiating spokes *between* each flower. This reinforces the design, yet softens the severe lines of the stems.

First, stick the skyrocket and firecracker in the floral foam. Then place *all* the red carnations on the left-hand side of the arrangement.

Next, place all the white carnations. You may have to adjust a few flowers later, but place them all now to create a solid band of a single color.

Finally, finish the bouquet with all of the blue carnations. This is a tinted flower, and the deeper the tint, the better. Maintain a triangle shape.

Add a few sprigs of myrtle or boxwood. Even Scotch broom would be satisfactory. Use just enough to separate the flowers and add a touch of green.

*D*esign can consist
of color arrangement as well as the form
into which flowers are placed.
In this Fourth of July bouquet, the red,
white and blue carnations must be maintained
in solid color blocks, because the red, white and blue are
fundamental symbols of the holiday.
When these three colors are
combined in a flower arrangement,
backed up by a reproduction
of the Declaration of Independence, we are
forcefully reminded of that day
in 1776 when democracy got its first
real working start.

Design Delight ... pages 24 and 25

ine flowers

could be hard to arrange —— if you didn't have a plan.

Planning is fundamental to a happy result.

And it surely applies to flower arranging.

Climbing up the ladder of learning, here are nine carnations

arranged in one way.

As you wander through the pages of this book,

you will discover there are dozens of other ways.

This bouquet is a classic example of nine carnations arranged in a triangle. The first three flowers establish the outside dimensions of the arrangement.

The next two flowers continue the triangle shape. Generally, it is easier to place the tallest flowers first, because they go into the center of the frog.

Add the flowers at the base of the arrangement. Continue to carry out the triangular form although you don't have to follow the placement shown exactly.

Now, place the foliage. Some foliage may be added earlier, but it is generally easier to create the effect you want if most foliage is added last.

*W*hat is your vision

of a crescent? A silver moon just beginning

its ascendency into fullness?

A flaky roll served with your continental breakfast?

The curved eyelid of your child, asleep and at peace?

Whatever your vision is, this is one of the loveliest of shapes ...

the bend in the river, turn in the road, arch in a willow tree,

the dappled shadow of a wave just before it crests

and breaks —— a curve —— a crescent.

Here you see it in flowers.

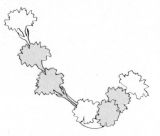

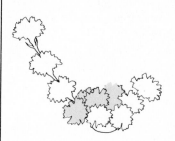

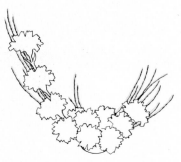

Select a flower with a relatively curved stem for the upper flower and fix it firmly in the frog. Place the lower two flowers to begin forming the crescent shape.	Next, place two more carnations with curved stems along the stem of the longest flower and two next to the bloom on the right-hand side.	Fill in the base of the bowl with four flowers, carefully maintaining a crescent outline for the arrangement. Your eye will tell you when it is right.	Place a naturally curved foliage such as Scotch broom in the arrangement to reinforce this crescent shape. Step #4 may be performed as step #1 if you wish.

Design Delight ... pages 28 and 29

   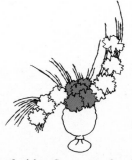

This Hogarth line arrangement is unique, because the Scotch broom foliage is placed first. The curve in the foliage establishes the line of the flowers.

A wire is pushed two inches through the top flower calyx, bent over, and the balance wrapped down the stem –– then curved to bend the flower stem.

The same procedure is followed with the lowest flowers. Other flowers are placed to form the lower "S" curve line which is shown in step #2.

The final four flowers are placed at the base of the bowl. Be careful to maintain the "S" shape by keeping these flowers close together in the "S" outline.

*T*he English painter, Hogarth,
called the "S" curve, as it occurs in nature and art,
his "line of beauty" and, thereby,
gained immortality for himself and coined a new adjective
for whatever art forms use this shape.
The Hogarth curve is particularly pleasing in floral arrangement
and provides an elegance and intrigue to the eye
which never loses its charm.

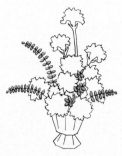

Place the tallest three carnations firmly in the pin frog. Utilize the natural curve in the stems as shown –– two to the left and one to the right.

Add flowers below the first three, again using the natural curve of the stems to reinforce the arrangement shape. Anchor securely in the pin frog.

Fill in the arrangement base with three more flowers. Stems of these carnations will not show so you need not be so concerned about how they curve.

Spray paint some spiral eucalyptus in a purple color that complements the blooms. Add a few shoots to finish off the arrangement as shown.

*M*onochromatic arrangements
can be exotically beautiful.
This study in purples makes the point.
From purple candle to purple flowers, it breathes an elegance
that only a single color in many shades can achieve.
The carnation variety is "Orchid Beauty" noted for its
spice-sweet, clove-like perfume –– the true carnation fragrance.
The spiral eucalyptus foliage has been sprayed
a pale purple to harmonize with the flowers
and the accessories.

Design Delight . . . pages 32 and 33

This arrangement is an inside circle of carnations surrounded by a half circle of carnations. Establish the arrangement height and width with three flowers.

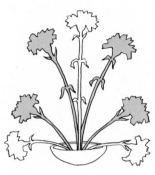

Next, finish the circle with four flowers. The stem length and placement of these carnations are critical, because even slight variations mar the bouquet's symmetry.

Place the small circle of carnations down in the bowl itself. These are very short-stemmed and placed in a round shape to cover the frog.

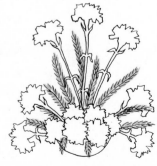

Add a few pieces of myrtle or other linear foliage which repeats the radiating pattern of stems coming out from the center circle of flowers.

*T*his picture

is a study in patterns.

Lights, bright dotted stars of light on one side ...

circles of light on the other.

Different ... yet reflecting the same patterned shape.

The flower arrangement is part of the pattern, too.

A circle of color crowning a center circle

of golden carnations ... a tasteful complement

to the many–circled background.

Design Delight ... pages 34 and 35

This monochromatic bouquet of green and blue tinted carnations is informal and off-center in shape. Place the first six flowers as shown.

Next, add flowers beside the top flower. Keep the arrangement effect informal by separating flower heads from each other with plenty of stem length.

Fill in the lower right and left sides of the bouquet. You may also want to add several flowers to the base at the back to make the arrangement two-sided.

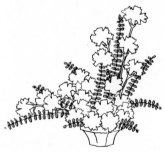

Add spiral eucalyptus foliage. This should fill in areas between stems, cover the frog and stems in the base of the bowl, and carry out the arrangement line.

Symphony in blue and green!
Tinted carnations, properly combined and placed
in the proper setting, make for highly unusual bouquets.
This L-shaped arrangement combines blue-green
carnations with dark blue, medium blue
and an aqua against a blue background.
Tinting solutions contain flower food
as well as preservatives which keep the carnations
as fresh and lovely as those
of natural color.

Design Delight ... pages 36 and 37

*S*ome containers

which will actually hold flowers are better used

as accessories to accompany an arrangement in another container.

Here is a case in point.

The exotic shapes of these blue Swedish glass bottles

would be much less effective

were they to be used with flowers in them.

And the arrangement of chartreuse carnations

sets them off to perfection.

   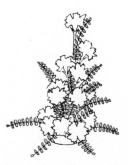

This conical arrangement is the same height as the tallest glass bottle. Place the top four flowers in a descending, circular pattern.	Add five more flowers beneath the first four. Use several pieces of fine wire to hold stems together if they tend to separate too much.	Fill in the base with seven more short carnations. The bowl edge will help you maintain the circular line for these flower heads.	Add spiral eucalyptus. You can be pretty casual about how this foliage is placed so long as it is evenly distributed.

Design Delight ... pages 38 and 39

To make this L-shaped arrangement, place the first three flowers as shown. The short carnation relieves the severity of the design.

Continue the vertical and horizontal lines of the bouquet with four more flowers. Add one short carnation on the right-hand side.

Fill in the center of the bouquet. Be careful to maintain a right angle arrangement shape by keeping flowers compact in the center.

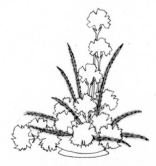

Green the bouquet with a spear-like foliage. Separate the flowers with the foliage, but be careful not to obscure or cover them up.

*D*ifferent floral accents
are possible to achieve using the many colors available
in tinted carnations. This coral carnation
arrangement suffuses its setting with a soft pink glow
that warms even the formal gold-striped
wallpaper background. Because
of their unusual color, these flowers would be equally
effective against a panelled wall,
a deeptone drapery or a textured divider screen.

Design Delight ... pages 40 and 41

Arrange this bouquet in descending tiers. The first flower is in the center of the pin frog. The next three circle the top flower. Hold them together with a small wire.

Five flowers circle the three above with stems in a circle in the pin frog. Be sure the vertical distance between flowers is the same. Hold these five with a wire.

Seven flowers form the bottom tier encircling the five above. No wire is needed here, because the lip of the bowl holds them together.

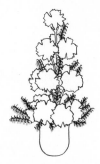

Add greens. Myrtle is used here, because it is delicate and lacy. It is easy to separate flowers in order to insert the foliage in the arrangement center.

*P*agodas whisper
romantic songs about the mystery of the Orient.
So, to give a Far Eastern flavor to an arrangement,
why not shape it like a pagoda?
This arrangement is one more example of the freedom of expression
which is yours in flower arrangement as an art form.
Once again, if you like it, it is lovely!

Design Delight ... pages 42 and 43

Arrange the top three flowers. Be sure the two side flowers are evenly spaced on either side of the tallest flower so that this bouquet becomes circular.

Then, arrange the next three flowers. Once again, be very careful that the placement of each bloom preserves the circular (or oval) shape of the design.

Place the last two flowers at the bottom of the arrangement. These flowers will complete the circle (or oval) shape so their position and length is important.

Add pieces of spiral eucalyptus. The reasons for foliage are to separate flowers, add depth to the design and put variation into the color pattern.

*J*apanese flower arrangements
make use of Japanese bowls like the ones in this picture.
They follow rigidly prescribed rules for their shape,
style and number of elements.
This arrangement is not in the Japanese style.
Rather, it is conventional,
but a bit on the unusual side,
because it is circular in shape and two-dimensional.
In other words, it is finished on the front side
only and intended for placement against a wall.
Once again, behold the elegance of simplicity.

Design Delight ... pages 44 and 45

*W*hat kinds
of accessories go with carnations?
Candle holders and candles, candy, fancy cakes,
ash trays, cigarette boxes, single flowers, leaves, pill boxes,
pictures, antique firearms, figurines, books, trays, keepsakes, wall hangings,
personal treasures. The infinite variety of objects
which can be used as accessories with flowers shows
us the truth at last – everything goes with flowers.

Color contrast and an informal arrangement shape which echo the shape of the butterfly are the keys here. Place the first three flowers as shown.

The next three flowers are put in place in a loose pattern around the tallest flower stem. Keep these blooms well separated from each other.

Add the five flowers to the bottom of the arrangement. There is also one short carnation placed in the back although you can't see it here.

Now, green it up with some huckleberry. Only **a** few sprigs are needed to separate flowers, hide stems and cover up the floral foam in the bowl.

Design Delight . . . pages 46 and 47

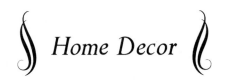

Home Decor

Mirrored beauty!

What a marvelous device a mirror is!

The faceless silvered face —— a tireless, impassive and

passionately truthful reproducer of every object that comes

within its range.

This antique Spanish mirror has reflected,

but left unrecorded, the passing of fascinating pages in history.

Now it reflects the beauty of a carnation arrangement

in an antique ruby glass sugar bowl.

What lovely image will it be privileged to reflect tomorrow?

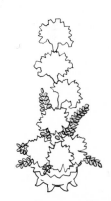

Floral foam serves as a frog in the ruby glass sugar bowl. The horizontal line arrangement is started with placement of the top flower and then the bottom two carnations.

Two more carnations are added. The tallest one is cut to a length which divides the distance between the top and the bottom flowers.

The last two flowers are placed as shown to form a vertical line. Note how beautifully the pale pink carnations go with the leather table base.

A few branches of spiral eucalyptus foliage are placed in the flowers. Use only small twigs, as larger branches would destroy the delicate grace of the bouquet.

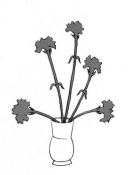   

The first five flowers establish the outline and general shape of the arrangement. By making the outline slightly irregular, the bouquet is given an informal style.

Add three more carnations. Keep them separated from other flowers, but maintain irregular arrangement shape so that the bouquet is asymmetrical.

Add five more flowers to the arrangement base. Because no two flowers are ever alike, your arrangement may look slightly different from this one.

Add myrtle foliage to relieve the hard lines of the carnation stems. Incidentally, myrtle has a refreshing, delicate fragrance which clings to your hands.

There's something regally beautiful
about Danish ware that fits it perfectly for carnation arrangements.
The muted colors, unusual glazes and textures,
and lovely shapes of containers, figurines and accessory pieces
add grace notes to every type of floral design.
This informal arrangement of tangerine carnations echoes
the color of the teak table, the vase decoration
and edge of the snuff box.

Home Decor ... pages 50 and 51

This informal vertical arrangement is another example of the beauty that can be yours with only seven carnations. Place the first three flowers as shown.

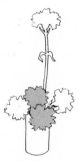

Next, fill in the bottom with two more flowers. The taller of the two flowers is placed toward the left side to begin the off-balance arrangement style.

Add the final two flowers on the left side. Much of the charm of this arrangement lies in the fact that it is not symmetrical and, therefore, intrigues the eye.

Foliage is added to separate the flowers. Once again, the weight of the foliage is kept on the left side to preserve the asymmetrical bouquet style.

This black cat figurine is a provider of good luck when it accompanies a lovely vase of yellow carnations. Although naturally yellow carnations are available, most yellow varieties do not grow well, and quantities are very limited. Therefore, white carnations are tinted by placing them in a yellow dye solution which goes up the stem and into the petals of the flower. They keep as well as untinted carnations, and the tinting process makes possible carnation colors not obtainable in nature.

Home Decor ... pages 52 and 53

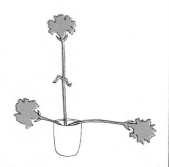  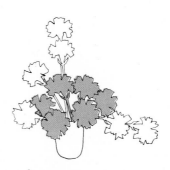 

This bouquet is an off-center triangle design. This offers a shape which provides informality in the finished arrangement. Place the first three flowers.

Add three more flowers as shown. Anchor these flowers carefully. Because this is a small container, the arrangement must be watered frequently.

Place the last six flowers. While this placement can be fairly loose, you must remember to maintain an approximation of the triangle shape.

Add camellia foliage. Here the large leaves are used to buttress the triangle shape and fill out the arrangement, while separating the flowers from each other.

Variegated carnations
are one of nature's prettiest whimsies.
Sometimes, the variegations occur as peppermint stripes
on a carnation petal having a solid color ——
sometimes as a color fringe ——
or even as bright color pencilling on a white background.
Here, variegated carnations are arranged and set against
a playroom wall —— a pleasing use
which picks up and reemphasizes the pleasant purposes to which
the room is dedicated.

Home Decor ... pages 54 and 55

lowers in a home

say something special to every guest who visits.

The message is a warm blending of "Welcome,"

"We are honored by your presence,"

and "Please partake of our hospitality."

There is no other way to make your joy in welcoming friends

more meaningful, more sincere.

This bouquet is shaped like an irregular triangle. Place the top and the two horizontal flowers as shown. A pin frog is used here as flower holder.

Add the center flowers below the top flower. Place one flower along the line established by the longest horizontal carnation on the left.

Fill in the center of the arrangement with six more flowers to cover the lip of the bowl and to hide the pin frog and bottom of flower stems.

A spear-like foliage is used for the main body of flowers. The darker, heavier leaf provides an accent at the top and bottom of the flower arrangement.

*T*he comfort of a fire ...

and man's intrigue with it ...

is so old that our friendly associations

with fire are almost a form of instinct.

A fireplace, ablaze with a pattern

of dancing light means shelter,

freedom from the cold, the warmth of friendship.

The bright color of a tangerine carnation

bouquet on a coffee table echoes the orange tongues

of flame. Can you think of a better

place to spend a quiet hour?

Home Decor ... pages 58 and 59

This asymmetrical arrangement must be in proportion to the height of the footed bowl. Place the first four flowers.

Now add more flowers to the vertical and horizontal arrangement lines, keeping the blooms slightly separated.

Add three final flowers at the base of the bowl. Insert stems of these carnations deep into the floral foam.

Green the bouquet. A few sprigs of myrtle foliage work ideally here, because its shape reinforces the floral design.

The regal nature
of carnations is revealed in their formal
Latin name — Dianthus Carophyllus — freely translated
as "Flower of Zeus" or "The Divine Flower
with the Scent of Clove."
In a formal container such as this Wedgwood urn,
formally arranged and placed in a formal setting,
elegance is the inevitable result.

This Wedgwood urn has a very narrow neck. Strip off all foliage so that stems will go inside the bowl. Place the first five flowers.

The arrangement shape is oval so the next five flowers are used to achieve this shape in the top two-thirds of the bouquet.

Place the bottom three flowers on the lip of the urn, but do not let them overhang so as to interrupt the container shape.

Add huckleberry foliage. Use it to separate flowers and fill gaps between flowers. Keep all foliage inside the bouquet outline.

Home Decor ... pages 60 and 61

Pewter furnishes a splendid texture

and surface for setting off the beauty of carnations.

This holiday bouquet of red carnations utilizes an antique pewter

ale tankard as a container.

Flanked by two pewter dishes, it sits on a fireplace mantle

in front of a mahogany wall.

As an added fillip, an old-fashioned pewter "wine taster" rests beside it,

but its rosy contents this time are a carnation bloom floated

in a small amount of water to keep it fresh and lovely.

Little things, such as this idea,

turn an ordinary bouquet into a conversation piece your guests

will long remember.

| This tankard is somewhat difficult to arrange because of the hinged lid. The first three flowers are placed with bottom flowers away from the container lid. | Two flowers are placed next to the tallest flower. This step is second, because to anchor these flowers firmly, you must be able to see the frog. | Fill in the bottom of the arrangement with four more flowers, keeping the mass effect of the blossoms as a counterbalance to the mass of the lid. | Add huckleberry to separate blooms, to add some green, and to lighten the effect of the arrangement. And, put one carnation in the wine taster. |

Home Decor ... pages 62 and 63

A pin frog is used in this bowl, because it is easily concealed in the bottom of the bowl. Place the two top flowers as shown with stems close together.

Place the next three flowers so that a vertical line is maintained for the arrangement. Exact flower length and position are important for good appearance.

Fill in a base of carnations for the arrangement. Be careful not to hide ends of the container, because they are important elements in the beauty of the bowl.

Add a few shoots of Scotch broom or other linear foliage. Be sparing, as too much embellishment would detract from the flowers as well as the bowl.

Siamese wedding bowls
are so beautifully hand decorated
and come in such graceful shapes that they are well worthy
of being photographed by themselves,
devoid of such embellishments as flowers.
Filled with carnations, however,
they become treasures befitting an emperor.
Here, white carnations bask in the splendor of warm sunshine
coming through a window in the late afternoon.
What a versatile home furnishing accessory flowers are!
How well they go with every decor!
To use them once, is to love
and use them ... forever.

Home Decor ... pages 64 and 65

Milady's Domain

When a mirror

reflects a lovely image, it doubles the visual pleasure

of the beholder.

What a simple device it is to place

a flower arrangement directly in front of a mirror!

An uncluttered wall covered with a muted wallpaper

becomes a "vision" with the addition

of five carnations in a small vase ——

reflected in an angular mirror.

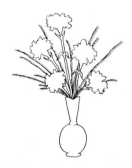

Although this container holds plenty of water, only a few flowers will go through the tiny hole in the top. Place the tallest flower first, as shown.

Place the two lowest flowers. Remove lower foliage so the stems will go down into the bowl. No frog is needed, because stems will fit so tightly together.

Place the fourth and fifth flowers to fill in the upper part of the arrangement. Once again, remove lower foliage so that stems will go into the bowl.

Finally, a few sprigs of Scotch broom fill in the empty spaces between flowers and soften the severe simplicity and lines of the floral design.

Pages 66 and 67

This vertical arrangement uses a small brass bowl. Flowers are placed alternately right and left down the entire vertical length of the bouquet.

Add three more flowers — left, then to the right, then left. Most carnations bend slightly one way or the other, so use the natural stem line.

Add three more flowers. Because this is a very feminine use for carnations, the last, short flower is placed out to the left to soften the arrangement line.

Add a few stalks of myrtle to the arrangement. Preserve the vertical line of the blooms by keeping foliage close to the stems. Use it sparingly.

arnations are

as much at home in a feminine boudoir

as they are on an executive's desk in a business office.

This versatility results as much from

their fragrance (always spicy but never cloying)

as from their gay colors and inviting flower form.

Wouldn't an arrangement like this

look beautiful on your boudoir table?

Milady's Domain ... pages 68 and 69

*W*hite *flowers*
in a white vase on a white background!
This treatment projects a delicacy in art equalled
only by the fragile beauty of the carnation petals themselves.
Two alabaster eggs,
limpid as two drops of oil suspended in water,
repeat the egg shape of the vase
which holds the arrangement.

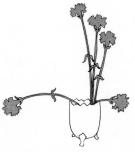

This unusual arrangement has three elliptical curves on its sides and bottom. Place the first five flowers as shown in saturated floral foam.

Place the next four flowers so that the flowers' heads form the ellipse on the left-hand side. Stem length and placement are critically important.

Place the last six flowers to form an ellipse on the right-hand side. At the same time, maintain an elliptical line across the bottom of the arrangement.

Now, add a linear foliage. Boxwood is shown here. A foliage with large leaves would suppress the lines of the arrangement, so a delicate foliage is better.

 hink of a

brass pitcher for watering houseplants as pretty as
Aladdin's Lamp, and then you'll have the container shown here.
Milady had eight gold carnations,
looked for a place to put them, saw her brass water pitcher,
and you see the happy result just after it was finished
on the work room bench.

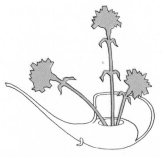

The trick here is to keep the carnations in place. Compressed chicken wire inside the container acts as a frog to hold the first three flowers.

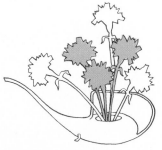

The stems of the next three flowers are inserted firmly into the loops of the chicken wire inside the container, deep down into the water.

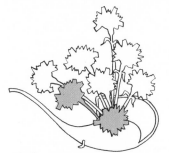

The last two carnations are placed. They are last, because holding them in a lower position requires the chicken wire loops plus the stems of the other carnations.

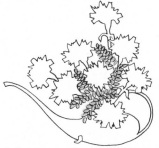

A few sprigs of leather leaf foliage are placed in between the flowers to fill in open spaces and cover the chicken wire inside the brass watering pitcher.

This upright triangular arrangement contains one dozen carnations. The first three flowers are placed in a tight, upside-down "T" to avoid dwarfing the bowl.

Four flowers are positioned around the tallest flower in a descending triangle. Keep the bouquet informal by breaking the triangle shape a bit.

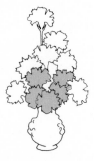

Add four carnations to the bottom. Keep them above the bowl somewhat so that the lovely texture and pattern of the Belleek is not hidden by flowers.

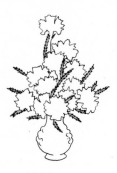

Add myrtle foliage. Separate the flowers with it, but use it sparingly to avoid a bushy or scraggly appearance in the final arrangement.

The beauty of a Belleek vase is heightened by a bouquet of pink carnations arranged inside it. Here the flowers echo the warmth and color of a marble topped table. A small Belleek seashell holds one carnation head floated in a small amount of water as a decorative accessory.

Milady's Domain ... pages 74 and 75

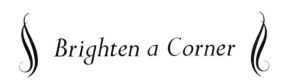

Brighten a Corner

*F̲lowers are usually
placed "on" something or "against" something.
When they are suspended in mid-air,
they achieve an ethereal grace which arrests and delights the eye.
This "flowers-in-a-basket" arrangement,
hanging from an almost invisible nylon fishing line,
floats like a lovely satellite in the sky.*

Wrap saturated floral foam in green foil. Place in basket set on work table. Arrange upper six flowers as shown. Stick stems right through the foil.

Next, with basket still on the table, place the next five flowers in the middle area. By cutting stems on a slant, they will pierce the foil easily.

Hang the basket on a nylon monofilament line. Add the lower flowers to counterbalance the basket. Keep stem holes in the foil small to avoid leaks.

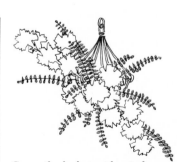

Green the basket with spiral eucalyptus. Greens are important to this arrangement, because they help to create the light, airy feeling the bouquet must have.

Pages 76 and 77

*H*appy holiday!
A giant brandy snifter never looked better
than with pink carnations filling its capacious interior.
This handsome arrangement would be beautiful anywhere
you put it –– console table in the hall,
coffee table or dining table.
It's not too tall or wide to look around.
It will stay fresh and lovely an unbelievably long time,
because the container holds in the humidity the flowers need
for maximum longevity.

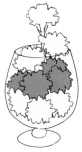

Place the top three flowers. The second flower should be just above the bowl rim, and the third just below it. A pin frog is used.

Now, arrange very short carnations around the bottom of the bowl. This must be done while you can still get your hand down into the bowl.

Next, place the intermediate flowers above these bottom flowers. You will need only three or four flowers here with fairly short stems placed in an upright position.

As a last step, add a few twigs of huckleberry, making sure that the foliage peeps out between individual blossoms, but does not dominate any area.

Brighten a Corner . . . pages 78 and 79

*G*reen *foliage plants*
make a marvelous backdrop against which to
place carnation arrangements.
Foliage plants and flowers are completely compatible.
This old-fashioned fern is perfectly suited to the lovely leaded
glass bowl and the pink blooms inside it.
The bouquet would go equally well with philodendron,
ivy, scheffleria or any of the many other foliage favorites
of both this and bygone days.

This bouquet is circular to fit the circular footed bowl. Place the first carnations as shown, keeping the stems of the bottom flowers in the very edge of the pin frog.

Next, add the flowers to the upper part of the bouquet. Place them in a circular pattern around the top flower, but keep them out away from it.

Add two or three flowers down inside the arrangement. By having shorter flowers inside longer ones, the illusion of arrangement depth is created.

Green the bouquet. Huckleberry is used here because of its small, attractive, bright green leaves. Also, it effectively covers the frog and hides stems in the bowl.

Brighten a Corner ... pages 80 and 81

This informal flower design is extended to the right of the bowl. Place the first three flowers as shown. Left flowers should be quite short.	Add flowers to the top and the right side of the arrangement. Preserve the informal shape by massing more flowers on the left than on the right.	Now fill in the bottom of the design to the right side. This balances the flowers placed to the left in step #2 and keeps the bouquet from being lopsided.	Green the bouquet as shown. Greens should maintain the informal lines of the arrangement and be used sparingly as an accent to the orange blooms.

For dramatic effect in a room,
the most striking color combinations result
when flowers of a color complementary
to the furnishings are used.
Complementary colors
provide a pleasing color contrast.
Thus, orange flowers against a green or blue wall
provide an electric color combination
so brilliant that it instantly attracts the eye.
Try the technique of putting complementary colors together
on your next flower arrangement.

Brighten a Corner ... pages 82 and 83

Flowers in a study
add to the comfort of a room designed
for the pleasant pursuits of reading, writing,
working and playing quiet games.
A pause in the occupation of the moment
is the more rewarding when one's attention can turn
to the beauty of a carnation bouquet placed
on a nearby table.

Although this informal bouquet is tall, it is designed for a small table. The first three flowers are fixed firmly in the frog as shown.

The next four flowers are arranged next to the top flower. Because this arrangement is tall, place these carnations firmly.

Add the last five flowers to the bottom of the arrangement. Keep it fairly shallow so that it will not overlap the small table top.

Add a narrow spike-like foliage such as myrtle. Use the foliage to soften the hard lines caused by stems and to conceal the frog.

Brighten a Corner ... pages 84 and 85

*M*ost of the arrangements

in this book have been placed in a particular setting.

When this bouquet in its lovely,

antique cut glass bowl was completed, however,

it seemed so beautiful that the time had come to present

flowers for flowers' sake. So, no setting is suggested.

This time, you are the interior decorator.

Where will you put it? On a buffet,

the piano, a coffee table, chest of drawers?

We think it will be beautiful anywhere.

Place the top flower and the ones down inside the bowl. The stems of these flowers inside the bowl should be fastened to the outer rim of the pin frog.

Place the next four flowers alongside the tallest stem. Stems of these flowers are stuck in the frog in a circle, around the tall center flower.

The last four flowers are placed around the center of the bouquet. This is a circular arrangement so it must look balanced and attractive from all sides.

Add greens between flowers as shown. They tend to soften the lines of the arrangement while adding a pleasing, complementary color which teases the eye.

Brighten a Corner ... pages 86 and 87

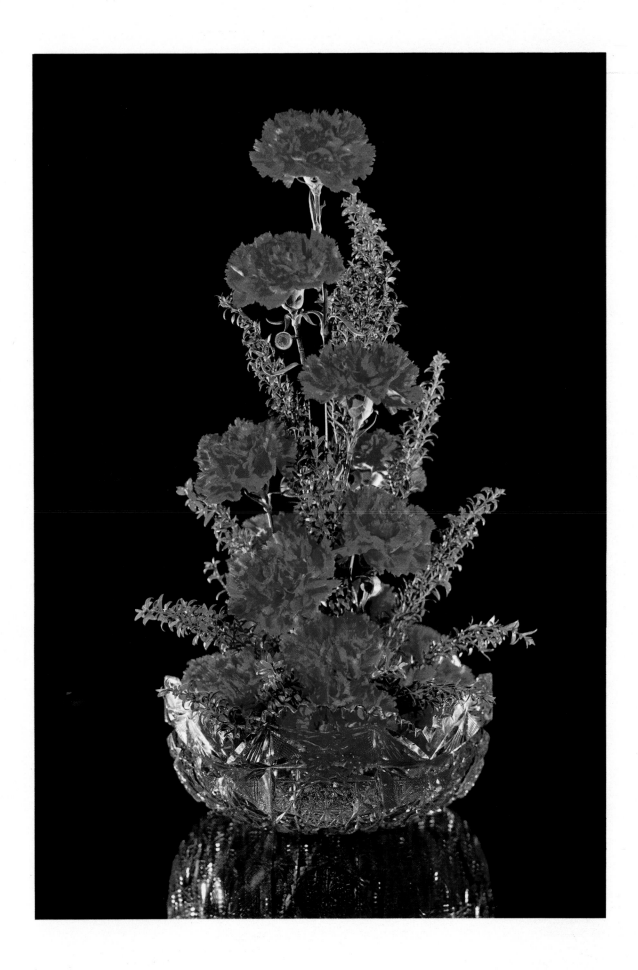

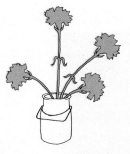

A pin frog is placed in the bottom of the mason jar. Because of the informality of the container, an informal circular arrangement shape is followed.

Add three more flowers as shown here. Preserve the circular shape by balancing off the flowers on the right side with the three new ones you add.

Add four more carnations to the bottom of the arrangement. Be sure the stems are secured in the pin frog so that the arrangement is sturdy.

Now, add foliage. Use a small, spear-like foliage rather than one with heavy, large leaves. This will help to preserve the identity of the rather unusual container.

) Bon Appetit (

*G*reat beauty is frequently
to be found in humble objects used for a decorative purpose.
An old-fashioned home canning jar with its rubber seal
and glass lid becomes an object of such beauty
when filled with carnations.
One can almost taste the gourmet salad
in the making which is placed beside
this floral accompaniment.

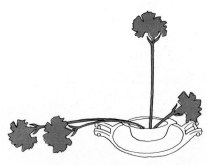

Place the first four carnations. The upright flower should be approximately two-thirds the length of the longest horizontal flower to keep the bouquet long and low.

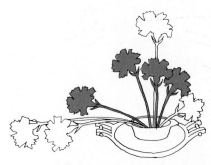

Add four more flowers to the center of the arrangement. These taller flowers should be placed in the center of the pin frog next to the top flower.

A right angle arrangement

doesn't have to be upright —

it can be low with a long,

horizontal sweep to it that fits a shelf,

window sill or a narrow table perfectly.

Here is just such an arrangement,

intended for use in the kitchen.

On a dinette or in a window sill,

it will brighten up every single moment milady

has to spend at her kitchen duties.

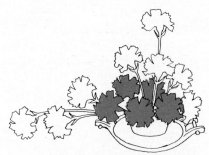

Finally, add the last five flowers around the bottom of the arrangement. Flower stems should never cross, but should radiate out from a center point.

Bon Appetit ... pages 90 and 91

Add a few sprigs of huckleberry. The green huckleberry foliage is particularly needed as a contrast color to the red flowers and the white bowl and trivet.

To hold the flowers, the pitcher has a small square of crumpled chicken wire inside of it. The first three flowers are tucked into loops in the wire.

Three flowers are next placed at the bottom of the arrangement, around the rim of the pitcher with the weight of flowers opposite the handle.

Place two more flowers around the pitcher's rim in similar positions to the flowers in step #2. This finishes up the back of the bouquet.

Finally, the last two flowers should be placed. It is easier to do these two last, because the other stems in the chicken wire insure firm support.

From the town of Vallauris in southern France comes a world-famous earthen ware. Here, in a little pitcher, while a soup cooking pot stands nearby, is an arrangement of tangerine carnations surrounded by the makings of a delicious Provençale soup. Kitchen accessories become decorative objects of art whenever they are used in this fashion as flower containers.

Bon Appetit ... pages 92 and 93

Do carnations fit the kitchen?
Very well, indeed, and especially when they are arranged
in a bright enamel teapot such as the one pictured here.
This arrangement is a combination of a vertical and a triangular shape.
Leather leaf adds just the touch of green
the brightly patterned red teapot needs.
You couldn't have a more cheerful accessory for your kitchen
than this bouquet sitting on a tabletop or counter.

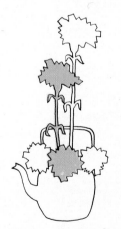

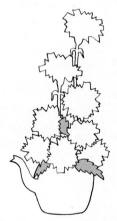

First, fill the teapot with foam and place the top and two outside carnations. A vertical design permits the shape and bright colors of the teapot to be seen.

Next, put a carnation between the two bottom flowers, and one longer stemmed carnation next to the top flower, keeping the stems close together.

Put the last three flowers in place. To finish the back, you need only to add one or two short carnations so that it may be viewed from either side.

Add a few pieces of green foliage. Foliage helps to separate the flowers and adds a pleasing green contrast to the red teapot and yellow carnations.

Bon Appetit ... pages 94 and 95

Place the middle carnations, the tallest and the widest in the arrangement. Keep it very low, because people must be able to see over the centerpiece to converse.

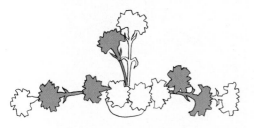

Place additional longitudinal carnations down the length of the table and one flower beside the center one. Be sure that the foam has a reservoir of water.

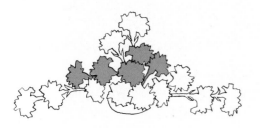

Fill in the bouquet center. Do both sides of the bouquet so that it is finished all the way around, because people will be seated on both sides of the table.

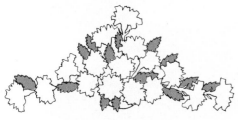

Now add evergreen foliage. Use it to separate flowers, cover the arrangement base, and add bright green color to the finished bouquet. Use it sparingly.

If you could have

a patio dinner in the most romantic place in the world,

where would you go?

How about a villa in the Italian Alps above Lake Como?

While steaks simmer on the charcoal grill,

tangerine carnations in a low,

linear arrangement glow with hot orange fire

that contrasts perfectly with the cool,

late afternoon colors of an Italian summer.

The good life couldn't be any better.

Bon Appetit ... pages 96 and 97

ea time

gets a floral lift with a bouquet of red carnations

echoing the beauty of a gleaming pewter coffee and tea service.

Small social occasions always assume

an added warmth when flowers are included as a decorative touch.

Tea time is a friendly occasion any time.

Flowers on the table make it more so.

| This triangular arrangement is formal in style and finished on all sides. The first three flowers set the bouquet's height and width. | The next flowers go around the top flower in a circular pattern to build the top of the triangle shape as shown. | Add flowers to the arrangement base, filling out the triangle with shorter carnations in a fairly tight pattern. | Add the greens. Salal (lemon-leaf) is used here between blooms, around the base and up at the top to form a green background. |

Bon Appetit ... pages 98 and 99

Window Pictures

*T*hanksgiving!

The holiday set aside to give thanks to the Almighty

for a bumper harvest.

How lovely is the party where the flower arrangement

which greets guests capsules the spirit of the season!

The flower container is a colorful squash. Foliage is red spiral eucalyptus.

Golden carnations repeat the bright colors of the fall woods,

and two ears of Indian corn complete the beauty of a setting

which would have pleased even the most severe

of our Pilgrim fathers.

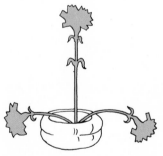 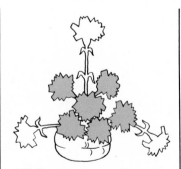  

Cut the top off of the squash, remove the seeds and insert saturated floral form. Add some water. Then place the first three carnations as shown.	Add five carnations to the center of the arrangement. At this point, the bouquet will be quite satisfying, and if you have few flowers, you can stop here.	For a fuller arrangement, five more flowers will make the bouquet much more impressive. Place them as shown, carefully maintaining a circular shape.	Red spiral eucalyptus foliage completes the arrangement. It is in perfect keeping with the fall motif, separates the flowers, and adds extra grace to the bouquet.

Pages 100 and 101

*C*arnations

in Manhattan —— a flaming bouquet of them on a

Park Avenue penthouse table against

the New York skyline.

This triangular arrangement uses myrtle foliage

and is placed in a handsome Swedish crystal vase.

What better way to set the stage

for a memorable penthouse party!

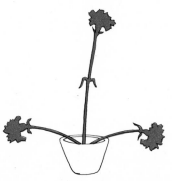

A block of floral foam is fitted into this Swedish glass vase. The top and two horizontal flowers are placed to establish the limits of the bouquet's triangular outline.

Additional carnations are placed beside the first three flowers to fill in and continue the triangular shape. Firm placement is essential to keep flowers from moving.

The bottom of the arrangement is completed by the addition of seven more blooms. The angular treatment emphasizes the geometrical buildings in the background.

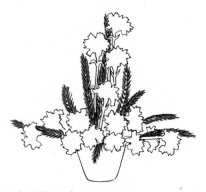

Myrtle foliage finishes the arrangement. It is used to separate flowers, cover the floral foam, and provide a complementary touch of green to the red carnations.

Window Pictures ... pages 102 and 103

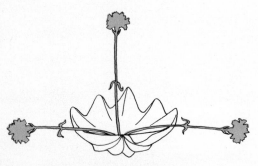

This arrangement requires that center flowers be kept low so that the outline of the shell container can be seen. Place the first flowers as shown.

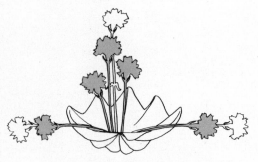

Add flowers in a low, horizontal line to both sides of the arrangement. Keep these flowers down so that the outline of the shell is preserved.

Put in three flowers beside the tallest flower. Keep the stems somewhat separated so that the shell flutes can be seen in the background.

Add the last two flowers. Keep them low. No foliage is used, as this would break the outline of the shell and make its shape difficult to identify.

*A big part
of the job of producing an unusual flower
arrangement can be accomplished through the
use of unusual containers.
This bouquet is placed in a giant clam shell.
Two pin frogs hold the flowers
so that the flutes of the shell can be seen.
Thus, the bouquet fits the
seaside setting perfectly.*

Window Pictures . . . pages 104 and 105

This bowl is three inches deep and from eight to ten inches wide. Carnation stems are shortened to four inches and placed in a circle around the bowl.

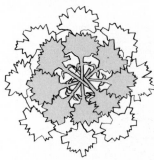

An inside circle of flowers with short stems is placed next to the outside carnations. No frog is necessary since flower stems rest on the bottom of the bowl.

*P*icture a floral powder puff!

A bright whimsy for a patio setting!

Gay color on a table! And so simple to do!

Here's a creative way for extending a few more days

of enjoyment from a bouquet whose days are coming to an end.

You need only a shallow bowl, short-stemmed

carnations, a touch of green.

Here's a bright floral star for your dinner table ––

it will shine in every guest's eye,

and yet they can all look over it

and converse with each

other beautifully.

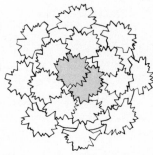

Two flowers in the middle finish it off. There should be at least one and one-half inches of water in the bowl at all times to keep the blooms fresh.

Small pieces of foliage are pushed into the water between flowers. You may need to lift several flowers up a bit to provide uniform arrangement height.

Window Pictures ... pages 106 and 107

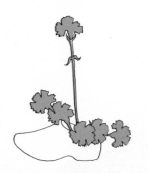   

Place the first six carnations in the pin frog as shown. Carnations should be up along the edge of the water container so as not to obscure the wooden shoe.

Add three more carnations. Remember, light carnations go to the top, darker color flowers to the bottom to form a solid color base for the arrangement.

Add the last two carnations to fill in the center of the arrangement. Keep the colors mixed —— with more light flowers to the top and dark at the base.

Add a light, leafy foliage. The bright green of huckleberry is perfect here for flower separation and optimum color contrast. Don't hide the shoe.

Holland is a world famous producer of flowers —— springtime tulips and hyacinths as well as a year 'round, continuous crop of roses, carnations, chrysanthemums and dozens of other flowers. So, here's a carnation arrangement in a Dutch wooden shoe on a window sill! May it be an appropriate recognition of the bright floral beauty which we enjoy every year in America, thanks to our hard-working, flower-growing friends in the Netherlands.

Window Pictures ... pages 108 and 109

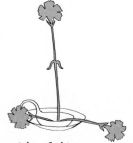

The weight of this arrangement is thrown to the right to balance the flowers against the birds. Place the first three flowers as shown, using a pin frog.

Additional flowers are added to the top and right side of the arrangement. Keep them toward the front, as the arrangement needs to be finished on one side only.

*G*old and pink create
a rich color combination which should be used
more often than it is. The graceful shape of the golden birds
sets them off against the gold bowl
and the gold fabric background. Placed beside a stained
glass window, the pink carnation
arrangement creates a beauty spot which would be the
pride of any homemaker's eye.

Add flowers to the arrangement with the greatest mass out along the right hand side of the bouquet's horizontal line. Keep the blooms toward the front.

Window Pictures ... pages 110 and 111

Add a linear foliage with narrow leaves. A bright green foliage is best, because it offers color contrast to the gold accessories and background.

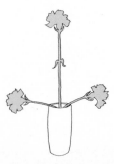

This arrangement has a half-sphere shape. A pin frog is secured in the vase. Place the first three flowers as shown.

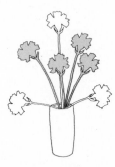

Add four additional flowers to the top. Stem lengths and placement must be precise to maintain the spherical shape of the bouquet.

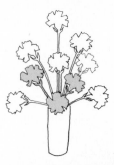

Insert the last three flowers. Keep them well separated from each other and so placed that they hold the half-sphere outline.

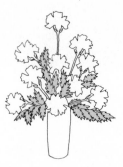

Add foliage to the arrangement to soften its lines, provide green contrast to the pink flowers and fill in bare areas between blooms.

*Do flowers enhance
or detract from a beautiful landscape seen through a window?
Judge for yourself in this mountain setting.
The antique Swedish vase filled with pink carnations
is a lovely part of your immediate surroundings.
When you look beyond,
the splendor of the mountain valley fills your eyes.
One view complements the other.*

Window Pictures ... pages 112 and 113

 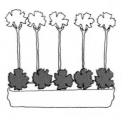  

Imagine a flower box planted with carnations. Then plant five carnations at regular intervals at the back of floral foam placed in your old planter dish.

Next, place five short carnations in the foam to the front of the planter. These should be lined up exactly with the tall carnations in the back.

Next, place the middle carnations in the middle of the box. Keep them exactly in line with the front and the back carnations as shown.

Now for the foliage – Scotch broom in the back between and behind the tall flowers – ivy between the middle and the short carnations at the base.

Nearly every household
has a small planter or dish garden vase
that is no longer being used. As a fun exercise,
here is one of these planters arranged like a window box.
Whether it were filled with tulips or geraniums
or carnations, it couldn't be prettier.
How well it would fit the square confines of a kitchen
or dining room inside window sill!

Festive Occasions

Carnations create
a stunning table centerpiece for formal parties or receptions.
The silver compote rises high enough above the table
on its footed base to leave room underneath it for candy,
cake or food placed around the arrangement.
Yet the flowers dominate the table
as they convey the unspoken message that this is
an occasion to remember.

Establish the arrangement height with one carnation somewhat taller than the bowl. Place horizontal flowers around the bowl like spokes in a wheel.

Fill in the top of the arrangement as if you were building a small chandelier – spokes of flowers out from the arrangement – some inside – in a regular pattern.

Add the last flowers to the bottom of the design. Again, put some inside, some outside, in a geometric, chandelier-type pattern around the compote.

Finally, relieve the severity of "flowers only" with a few sprigs of green. Use greens only to separate flowers and add a small amount of color.

Pages 116 and 117

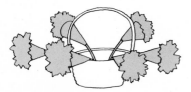

Cut six carnations to the same length. Remove bottom leaves and push through ice cream cones. Fasten cones to stems with adhesive tape and place in a low circle.

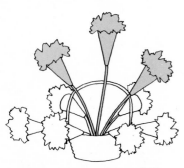

Follow same procedure with three longer stemmed carnations. Once again, tape cones to stems of flowers so that blooms are held in the cone cup.

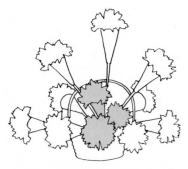

Fill in intermediate spaces with short-stemmed carnations. This hides the frog or floral foam used as a flower holder and gives the arrangement depth.

Add a few pieces of foliage. Be sure to cover the longer stems of the top flowers which look somewhat bare because lower leaves have been removed.

*H*appy Birthday!

To say it with flowers to a birthday child,
here's a special bouquet made with ice cream cones and
strawberry pink carnations arranged in a small basket.
How nice it would be to be a birthday child
once again!

Festive Occasions ... pages 118 and 119

 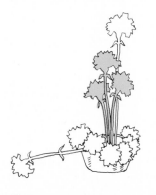 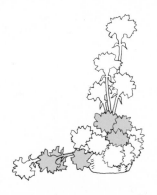 

Place a small ceramic bowl with floral foam in the bread basket and position the top and extreme left lower flower first. Then, add the other six flowers.	Add three flowers next to the tallest flower. Add two flowers along the left lower carnation. Fix stems firmly in the foam so that they stay in place.	Fill in the base of the arrangement with four more flowers so that the basket appears to be filled with flowers in an L-shaped arrangement.	Finish off the arrangement by filling in spaces between flowers with myrtle foliage or other suitable linear foliage having straight lines and a soft appearance.

*S*pring *is so beautiful,*
so full of summer's promises yet to be fulfilled,
small wonder that the older we get, the more we look forward to its coming.
So, let's have a springtime picnic in the backyard!
An L-shaped arrangement of yellow carnations in a bread basket
would put even a glum guest in a party mood.
What's in the basket? A gourmet picnic lunch to match
the splendor of the centerpiece.

Festive Occasions ... pages 120 and 121

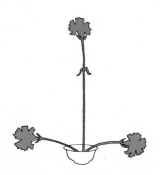   

This is a T-shaped rather than tri-angular arrangement. The first three carnations establish the height and width of the bouquet.

Additional flowers fill in the ver-tical and horizontal lines of the arrangement. Straight stems are essential in the vertical flowers.

Fill in the center of the arrange-ment. It should be slightly wider than the top flowers to form a base for the bouquet.

Add foliage. Quite a few sprigs may be used if it is delicate. Greens are important in breaking up the mass of the flowers.

Graduations are sentimental times.

A small girl, suddenly grown up,

is about to start on a new and different life.

It is a time for departings and beginnings.

How can one best express love and Godspeed to the graduate?

Nothing speaks your heart as well as a floral remembrance.

She will probably save and dry one flower

to be kept with such special other treasures as

the corsage she received on the day

of her engagement and a blossom from

her wedding bouquet.

Something old,
something new, something borrowed and something blue.
This bridal shower fulfills all these requirements —
an antique tablecloth, a new,
little wedding bells mobile, a borrowed vase and a blue background.
Because carnations are noted for their keeping quality,
long after the guests have gone,
the bouquet will offer the bride-to-be a handsome remembrance
of a lovingly happy occasion.

  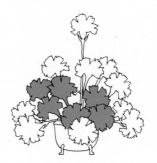 

This is a round bouquet. The top flower is placed in the center of floral foam while the bottom flowers radiate around it like spokes in a wheel.	The next four flowers are placed around the top flower. The bouquet is finished on all sides so these flowers must go *around* the center bloom.	Now, fill in the bottom center of the bouquet, adding carnations all the way *around* the bowl so that it looks finished all the way around.	A few shoots of leafy foliage fill in the spaces between flowers with pleasing, dark green color. Be sure to cover the floral foam with the greens.

Festive Occasions ... pages 124 and 125

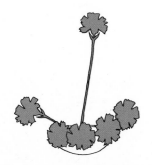   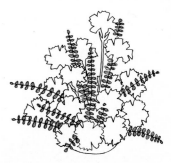

This bouquet is really a fan of carnations with just enough irregularity to be eye-catching. Place the first six carnations into floral foam as shown.

Now fill in the upper part of the fan with five more flowers. Keep the blooms separated loosely so that flowers don't overlap each other.

Next, the arrangement's center must be filled in with four more flowers. Be sure that a small reservoir of water surrounds the foam so that the flowers keep well.

Finally, add eucalyptus foliage to fill in spaces between flowers and to hide the foam. Like the flowers, the foliage must be in water to stay fresh and green.

Carnations and champagne!
Thoughtful the friend who provides
this kind of a bon voyage gift
to a lucky traveler and his wife.
A giant supersonic transport model symbolizes tomorrow's
air travel — while carnations and champagne
bespeak the fun and excitement of today's
unforgettable vacation.

Festive Occasions ... pages 126 and 127

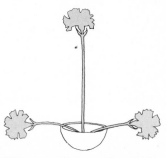

This arrangement is shaped like an isosceles triangle. The first three carnations establish the altitude and the base for the triangle.

Add five additional flowers to fill in the sides of the triangle. Be sure that flowers' stems radiate out from the center, and are placed in the center of the frog.

Fill in the triangle base. This baby shower bouquet with its blue accessories and pink flowers will fit the new arrival whether it be a boy or girl.

Add foliage between flowers to fill in open spaces and to cover the frog. Foliage stems should not cross the stems of the flowers, but radiate out from the center.

A baby shower
without flowers would be like a wedding
without rice to throw at the bride and groom.
These lovely pink carnations
are arranged in a blue bowl placed on a straw mat,
laced with dainty pink ribbon.
Pink and blue — girl or boy —
happy the mother-to-be
whose child receives this kind
of an early welcome!

Festive Occasions ... pages 128 and 129

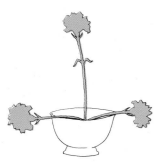   

Since this bouquet will be on a dining table, it must be low and should also be long and narrow. Establish height and width with three flowers.

Add carnations to the middle of the arrangement. Place these so as to achieve a fairly full effect inside the wide-mouthed Revere bowl.

Add carnations to the arrangement base. Be sure to finish the bouquet on all sides, as it will be viewed from every angle by your luncheon guests.

Add foliage — — camellia leaves, or lemon leaf (salal), to conceal the floral foam used as a frog and to fill in open spaces between flowers.

To set a most special table —

a luncheon to remember in a setting never-to-be-forgotten —

there is only one accessory

which can adequately wear the word "unique".

Flowers! No two are alike.

No two arrangements are ever the same.

No other accessory can instantly be changed

to fit the mood or need of your party. Wrong color?

Just add or change flowers in an appropriate

complementary color! Or, change the foliage or the bowl.

Wrong shape? Just lower the arrangement

or expand it or condense it.

Fresh flowers such as these say someone lives here

who loves you and who welcomes you

with nature's loveliest gift.

Festive Occasions . . . pages 130 and 131

This buffet table centerpiece is long, but need not be too low, because guests will not be looking across it while seated. Place the first five flowers.

The top center of the arrangement is filled in with five flowers. Because this bouquet is viewed from all sides, the back should be finished and symmetrical.

Now, give the arrangement a base with nine more carnations. Here again, finish the back as well as the front to preserve a symmetrical appearance.

Now add the foliage. The pleasing gray green color of spiral eucalyptus goes well with a bouquet of this sort and harmonizes nicely with the blue cloth.

*W*hatever etiquette
or party planning guide you check,
everyone that discusses a buffet
set-up carefully provides a place for flowers.
This formal buffet provides you with the reason why.
How austere this table would be without the comfort to the eye
which flowers provide! A bowl of fruit,
glass balls, figurine, even an ice carving
could not match the essence of beauty
which flowers have achieved.

Festive Occasions ... pages 132 and 133

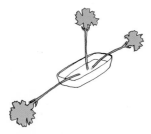

This arrangement must be low (so diners can see over it) and long (so it extends down the table). Place the first three carnations as shown.

Next, add vertical and horizontal flowers, keeping the lines of the flowers in the shape of a squat, equilateral triangle. Fix them firmly in the frog.

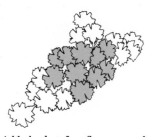

Add the last few flowers to the center of the arrangement on both sides. Keep the bouquet narrow so that it leaves space for china, crystal and silver.

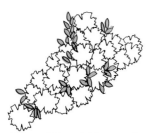

Add a small-leaved foliage such as huckleberry, using only enough to fill holes in the bouquet, cover the frog, separate flowers and hide the bowl.

Golden wedding anniversaries are proud moments for the lucky couple who have spent fifty years together. Golden carnations and golden flatware reflect the treasured character of a golden wedding dinner. The table wouldn't be complete without the beauty of this lovely floral centerpiece.

Festive Occasions ... pages 134 and 135

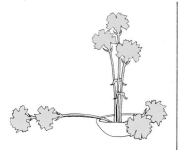

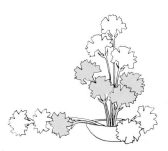

This is a big arrangement, using eighteen flowers. Since it sits in the corner of the tea cart, construction is started with seven flowers in step #1 as shown.

Next, add carnations to the main body of the arrangement, preserving the right angle L-shape by keeping center flowers in an upright line.

Add the rest of the carnations to the base. Once again, a linear, horizontal form should be followed to keep the arrangement from appearing too bushy.

Finally, add the foliage. Camellia foliage has been used to give the arrangement base more weight with a linear foliage for the upper part.

*F*or patio parties,

you, as the party planner, will gain

a special reputation for prettier party settings

if you make flowers an important part of every occasion.

Here, on a patio tea cart,

next to the lemonade, they help to make a good party even better.

On a July afternoon, lemonade is a cool idea —

enhanced and made even more cool with a lemon-colored

carnation arrangement.

Festive Occasions ... pages 136 and 137

Oriental Art

As an art form,
Japanese flower arrangements make use of natural materials,
using the natural line of the material in rigidly prescribed classical patterns.
It is possible, however, to give an arrangement a Japanese
feeling by using appropriate foliage, container,
accessories, and arrangement line. Pussy willows,
incense burner container, cricket, and a slanted, circular form
give this bouquet a light Oriental air.

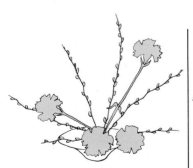

Four flowers *and* the longest pussy willows are placed first. Pussy willows and flowers are arranged on a slant to achieve an Oriental effect. Firm placement is essential.

The next four flowers are positioned to fill in the top of the arrangement and to carry out the slanting line of the bouquet. Be sure the flowers are firmly fixed.

Two last flowers are placed at the back to fill in the base. These cover the pin frog and provide some color as they are seen through the bouquet.

A few more short sprigs of pussy willow are added in amongst the carnations. Use slender branches rather than heavy ones to keep the arrangement airy.

Pages 138 and 139

The secret here is to keep the flowers at the bottom of the arrangement, inside the lip of the dish. Place the first six flowers as shown.

Add four more upright carnations next to the top flower. If necessary, hold these close to the main stem with a small piece of thread or wire.

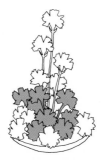

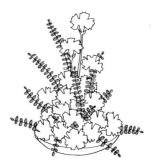

Add eight more carnations. These go all the way around the bottom, because the arrangement is circular and is intended to be viewed from all sides.

Now, a few sprigs of spiral eucalyptus finish the design. Although the flowers are kept inside the bowl, to break the bouquet's formality, the foliage extends beyond it.

Most flower arrangements
spill over the edges of the bowls that contain them.
This arrangement, in a very large, flat,
circular Japanese bowl, is unusual,
because all flowers, including the outside ones
which would normally go over the bowl edge,
stay inside it. The bowl must be filled with water every day
to keep the ends of the flower stems covered.

Oriental Art ... pages 140 and 141

Because the flowers must be worked in and around the branches, the dead twig of the tree is placed first. Stick it firmly into the needle holder.

Next, add the four flowers which set the outlines and limits of the arrangement. Work these through the branches of the twig so that they stand up straight.

Add the last three carnations. Once again, the stems should not be bent around the twig branches, but threaded through them and stuck into the holder.

Add a few sprigs of "Baby's Breath." This material is so dainty that practically any branch of it that you select will work beautifully in providing a graceful effect.

The rich texture of this brocade background makes the choice of an Oriental style arrangement both a natural and logical decision. A bare branch, the delicate tendrils and blossoms of "Baby's Breath," red carnations and a few green leaves around the base create a picture of arresting beauty. And yet, this beauty was created with very few flowers.

Oriental Art ... pages 142 and 143

   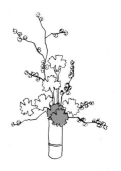

Fill the bowl with saturated floral foam. Then place two or three small branches of flowering purple plum toward the back of the bowl.

Add the first three carnations. Since the weight of the plum branches is to the right, the weight of the flowers will be to the left of the bouquet.

Add two more flowers to the left-hand side of the bouquet. This brings the branches and the blooms into balance as a floral composition.

Two more flowers go into the arrangement base – one in the front and one in the back. Because the vase opening is small, this covers the floral foam.

W hat," you may well ask,

"is an Oriental-style arrangement doing in a book where

no rules arrangements are the rule?"

It is true that no other arrangement style is surrounded by quite such

a mystique and requirement for carefully prescribed form as Japanese

arrangements. That's why this particular one is here.

If a pleasing Oriental feeling can be accomplished,

having simplicity of line and using natural materials, without an

over-concern for representations of Earth, Man and Heaven,

why not give it a try?

Oriental Art . . . pages 144 and 145

Happy Holidays

*H*aloween
—— the festive children's holiday when witches,
goblins and ghosts are about ——
provides an ideal occasion for a fall party.
To set the theme, here's a fresh pumpkin made into a
jack–o'–lantern flower container.
The accessories? Candy corn, cider, sandwiches if you like.
Or you can place a complete buffet supper into
this cheerful and charming setting.

Insert floral foam in the carved pumpkin and set the three cat-tails in place. Add three carnations to establish maximum height and width for the arrangement	Fill in with five more carnations. Work these flowers into the center and bottom of the arrangement keeping the design in proper balance and perspective.	Add five more carnations. Also place teasels in amongst the flowers to fill in empty spaces in the arrangement. Again, maintain balance in the flowers and teasels.	Finally, add three more teasels and one last carnation. Around the pumpkin top, place oak leaves to cover stems, floral foam, and the arrangement base.

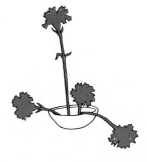

The first four carnations are placed as shown. For balance, the tallest flower should curve away from the longest flower at the bottom.

Five carnations are added. On the left side, stems curve the same direction as the top flower. On the right side, they curve the other way.

*T*raditional Christmas!

One of the reassuring qualities of Christmas

is its tradition. For hundreds of years,

we have been celebrating it joyfully –– an occasion

for enjoying all of the things which have become

Christmas symbols –– Santa Claus, Christmas carols,

the Christmas tree and flowers.

Here, a conventional arrangement of red carnations complements

the Christmas background

of an evergreen mantlepiece while red candles

symbolize the happy associations

which mean and are Christmas.

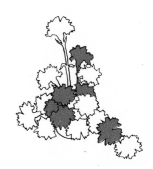

The last six carnations are placed to fill in and complete the informal shape of this arrangement. Water this arrangement frequently to keep it fresh.

Happy Holidays ... pages 148 and 149

A few branches of evergreen, in this case California redwood, add the green color which contrasts so beautifully with the red flowers for perfect Christmas color.

*A*lthough

it may be hard to believe,

this carnation Christmas tree is arranged

in a relatively small, round bowl.

Therefore, because it contains two dozen carnations,

it must be watered frequently (at least twice a day)

with a long-spouted watering pitcher.

Evergreen foliage adds an additional touch to the illusion

of a miniature Christmas tree created

with vibrant red carnations.

The bowl is filled with floral foam which is held in place with adhesive tape. The top three carnations are then placed close together as shown.

Next, the middle flowers are put in place. Because the bouquet is circular, the back must be filled in and a regular circular cone outline maintained.

The bottom flowers are now positioned. Although you can see only seven flowers in the drawing, eight more are needed to finish the sides and back.

Now, add the evergreen. Use it to separate flowers, but be careful not to make it too long and bushy or the bouquet will have a whiskery appearance.

Happy Holidays ... pages 150 and 151

 blue glass bowl – –

shaped like an Easter hat and filled with carnations – – produces

an Easter bouquet pretty enough to make

any heart happy at Easter time.

The wide variety of pastel, variegated

and tinted carnations suits them beautifully to Easter bouquets.

A little girl's Easter basket accompanies

this Easter hat full of flowers.

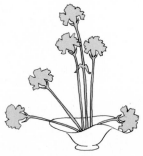

This Easter bouquet is placed in a blue bowl shaped like an Easter bonnet. Six purple and pink carnations are placed in a large fan shape.

Five more flowers are placed at the right center. Keep the light pink flowers to the top of the bouquet with the purple at the bottom.

Fill in the bottom of the bouquet with purple and pink flowers, using more purple than pink. This provides a color base for the arrangement.

Add foliage to separate flowers, soften the lines caused by stems, fill in holes between flowers, and to cover the frog and the base. Don't overdo the foliage.

Happy Holidays ... pages 152 and 153

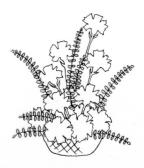

When an arrangement contains dark pink, lighter pink and yellow flowers, proper use of color requires that lighter colors be at the top. Place the top three.

Place the next three flowers. The basket is sprayed gold and has a small foam-filled bowl inside it to hold flowers and water. Keep the bouquet shape informal.

Next, add the five carnations to the bottom of the bouquet. You may vary the colors to suit yourself, but use more dark pink than light flowers at the base.

The foliage is spiral eucalyptus sprayed gold to match the two Easter baskets. Place it as shown between the flowers to add informality to the arrangement line.

Easter has such beautiful associations!
The Easter egg hunts we enjoyed as children,
the fun of coloring and decorating eggs!
The happy Easter rabbit!
And, the first flowers of Spring!
Here an Easter basket full of pink and yellow flowers
would be pretty anywhere with
or without its children's accompaniment of
Easter eggs and Easter rabbit.

Happy Holidays ... pages 154 and 155

*H*appy New Year!

Gay hats, serpentine confetti and carnations —

these are the accoutrements

of the good time that accompanies the passing

of the old year and the welcoming of the new.

A triangular arrangement shape fits

the flowers perfectly on a small corner table

in the corner of a room.

This arrangement is shaped like one-fourth of a cone. The top flower is upright with the two bottom flowers projecting forward to form a ninety degree angle.

The next four flowers continue the shape of one-fourth of a cone, projecting both up and forward. The arrangement is kept in this shape so it will fit in the corner.

The last two flowers are placed in the center, again projecting both up and out to complete the conical shape. Stem length and angle are critical.

Finally, huckleberry foliage is added to fill in spaces between flowers and to cover the floral foam which serves as a flower holder. Use foliage sparingly.

Happy Holidays ... pages 156 and 157

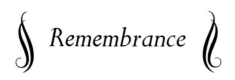 Remembrance

Establish the height and width of the arrangement with three flowers. To gain an informal feeling, this arrangement is asymmetrical in shape.

Next, add the two taller flowers that go beside the top flower. These should be placed on either side of the top flower, close together as shown.

 ld-fashioned charm
is never more evident than in a bouquet of carnations
arranged in a treasured antique vase.
These fragrant white blooms would serve
as a thoughtful Valentine, a birthday remembrance,
or a special "Thank You."
Happy would be the recipient of such a gift!
Good wishes are always underscored
when you "say it with flowers."

Add a flower to the bottom of the arrangement in the front. Add another flower to the back so that the bouquet is finished on all sides.

Soften the arrangement's lines with foliage to separate the flowers and complement the pink and red background and ruby glass of the container.

Pages 158 and 159

Mother's Day

was first promoted in 1908 when Anna Jarvis of Philadelphia
presented five hundred carnations to friends and neighbors
on the anniversary of her own mother's death.
This simple beginning ultimately resulted in the official
designation of the day by Congress in 1914.
The official Mother's Day flower
is the red carnation worn by those whose mothers
are living and white for those
less fortunate. Red carnations, like the ones in this
arrangement, are the official gift of the day
for every proud mother across the land.

  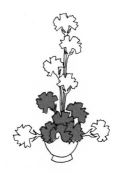 

| This vertical, triangular arrangement is formal in design. Place the first three flowers firmly in the frog as shown. | Add three flowers beside the top flower. Keep the stems close together. Use fine wire to hold stems together, if necessary. | Add the bottom flowers. Preserve the triangular shape and keep the flowers close together so that the bouquet has a good base. | Add a small amount of huckleberry to the bottom of the arrangement. Use it to separate flowers and to conceal the frog. |

Remembrance ... pages 160 and 161

This short, round arrangement requires a half-sphere form. Establish the height of the first flower. It will determine the length of all other carnations.

Cut the circumference flowers at the arrangement base to the same length as the first flower. Place these five flowers like the spokes in a wheel.

Next, place five flowers of the same length as the first halfway between top and circumference flowers and midway between the circumference flowers.

Fill in areas between flowers with ivy to cover up the floral foam, hide the bowl edge and conceal stems which interrupt the bouquet's form.

*W*hen a person thinks,
of one's mother and Mother's Day,
one instantly thinks of home.
And, of all the good things associated with home ...
comfort, security and good home-cooked meals.
Here, a Mother's Day arrangement,
placed next to such everyday accessories as cookbooks,
fruit prints and a wall covered
with green fabric, creates a scene to remember
with warmth and tenderness.

Remembrance ... pages 162 and 163

Because this container is unusual, special pains must be taken not to hide it. The first three carnations are arranged as shown. Keep the flowers up.

Add three more flowers beside the tallest carnation in the center. Once again, keep them well up so that there is room for the last four blooms.

Add four carnations. Please note that only the last two flowers break the line of the duck's back to hide the opening and the floral foam.

Add huckleberry to separate flowers and to add the sparkling contrast of bright green leaves against red flowers. It is one of nature's most pleasing combinations.

Some containers
are just made to order for certain types of occasions.
Thus, a bowl shaped like a hat is perfect for Easter ——
a ruby glass container is ideal for Valentine's Day ——
a pumpkin fits the Halloween or Thanksgiving scene.
This container, copied after a wild duck decoy,
has "Fathers' Day" written all over it.
And red carnations, the Fathers' Day flower,
make it an unqualified first choice
for a remembrance any father
would be proud to receive.

Remembrance . . . pages 164 and 165

ather's Day

is a wonderful time for carnation bouquets.

Carnations are as much a man's flower as they are feminine.

You may not be able to afford to give your father antique dueling pistols,

but carnations are within everyone's reach.

And they say "I love you" to him in a masculine way

that you may not be able to express in words.

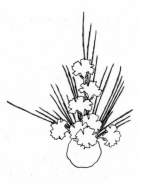

This triangular arrangement uses only eight flowers in a very simple geometric form. Place the first three flowers to set the outline of the arrangement shape.	Place two more upright flowers beside the main stem. Keep these flowers close together. A fine piece of thread or wire tied to the stems will be of help.	Add three flowers to the center and bottom part of the arrangement. The very bottom flower should extend out slightly over the front lip of the bowl.	Finally, it's time for the foliage. A few shoots of Scotch broom extend beyond the flowers, yet serve to reinforce the triangular bouquet shape.

Remembrance . . . pages 166 and 167

St. Patrick's Day
is the day of year dedicated to the color "green."
It is the day for green neckties,
green dresses, green candy, green shamrocks and,
above all, green carnations.
Our St. Patrick's Day party is highlighted
by a circular table centerpiece of green
carnations in a tiered arrangement.
Anyone for Irish coffee?

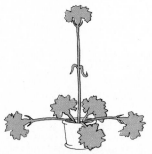

This table arrangement is conical in shape with the carnations arranged in tiers. Place the tallest flower and the bottom circle of flowers.

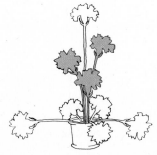

Next, arrange the tier of flowers around the tallest flower. Remember that the arrangement is viewed from all sides so a conical shape must be maintained.

Fill in the base with carnations. Keep some of the flowers very short and well into the middle of the bouquet, with others longer to give the arrangement depth.

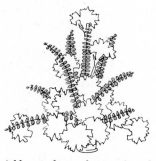

Add spiral eucalyptus for the softening effect which this foliage provides. Use the foliage also to create the illusion of depth in the bouquet.

Remembrance ... pages 168 and 169

Establish the height and width of the arrangement with three carnations. Because the bowl is small, be sure it is filled regularly with water.

Next, fill in the base with three more flowers. Because these carnations have very short stems and, therefore, little food, a floral preservative is a good idea.

Place the lower left and the upper right carnations to form a circular pattern. Be sure to leave enough room to insert the two additional flowers needed.

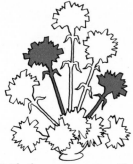

Finish the arrangement with the last two carnations. Precise flower length and arrangement is required for the circular outline which makes this bouquet attractive.

Happy Valentine!

One need not love Danish design to appreciate

the Valentine message contained in this floral tribute

to Valentine's Day.

Candle holders, candles, heart mobile

and even the small flower bowl are all of Danish origin.

In Denmark, hearts are Christmas decorations, too ——

the season when one expresses one's heart

and achieves the spirit of Christmas from one's heart.

How well these accessories also fulfill the Valentine message!

Wouldn't flowers be a wonderful way to say

"Happy Valentine" to someone you love?

Remembrance ... pages 170 and 171

*W*hat can anyone say
that is more important, more succinct, more meaningful
than, "I love you"?
St. Valentine's Day, set aside for lovers, is dedicated
to this belief in the power
of the sentiment expressed in these words. And how
can you say it more persuasively?
With flowers.

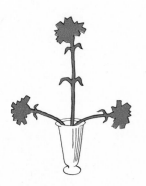

Fill the vase with a plug of saturated floral foam. Establish the height and width of the arrangement with three carnations in a triangular pattern.

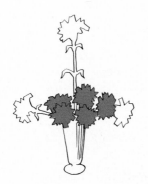

Fill in a cluster of carnations at the lip of the vase. Insert these carnations well into the foam so that they get enough water. Keep flower heads close together.

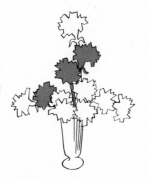

Place additional carnations along the stem of the tallest flower. Then, to fill out the triangle shape add one more flower on the left side.

Finally, add foliage around the bottom of the vase. Only a small amount is needed, because too much would overpower the small vase.

Remembrance ... pages 172 and 173

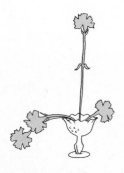   

This arrangement achieves a formal grace through its off-center design. Establish the limits of the design with four flowers placed in a frog as shown.

Add four more flowers down along the stem of the tallest carnation. Keep them close together but be careful to separate the blooms from each other.

Add five more shorter carnations to the bottom of the arrangement working them out to the left-hand side to fill in and complete the design.

Now add greens. Leather leaf is ideal because of its triangular form and compact green leaf. Use just enough to separate flowers and cover the pin frog.

Remembrance enjoys a special lift for the heart and spirit when it is symbolized in the beauty of flowers. Whether you are recalling a birthday or an anniversary, saying "Congratulations" or wishing a speedy recovery to a convalescent, the bright colors and beauty of carnations will give your expression new eloquence.

Remembrance ... pages 174 and 175

*F*lowers have always been,

and probably always will be, the sweetest way to say, "Sweetheart."

No other gift expresses so well the wordless thoughts and feelings of love.

The very nature of the gift — ephemeral, fragile and

yet beautiful — shows that regard has been put above price

and tangible permanence. As a remembrance of love,

flowers thus become one of Nature's

most persuasive messengers.

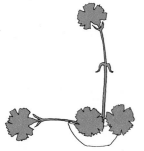

This right angle or L-shaped arrangement is relatively easy to make. A pin frog holds the flowers with the first four placed as shown.	Four more flowers begin to fill in and break up the severity of the right angle arrangement line with just enough variation to informalize the pattern.	Two additional flowers at the base cover the needle holder. Several additional flowers should go in the back if the bouquet is to be two-sided.	A few sprigs of huckleberry separate the flowers and add some green accents to the white arrangement placed against the red, quilted satin background.

Remembrance ... pages 176 and 177

Helpful Hints

Helpful Hints for Every Flower Arranger

1. *Water*

   Water is the lifeblood of all growing things, *and all cut flowers.*

   Until a cut flower "goes to sleep," it is as much alive as a green plant with roots in the ground. All cut flowers, and carnations are no exception, plus the green foliage used in flower arrangements, must have the ends of the stem covered with water.

   Deep water is preferrable to shallow water for carnations because it provides hydraulic pressure which forces the water up the stem of the plant and into the flower head.

2. *Flower Preservatives*

   Flower preservatives provide more life for cut flowers. They add two things. First, they provide food for the stem and for the flower head. Second, they inhibit the growth of algae and fungi in the end of the stem which prevent water from traveling up the stem to the flower.

   Some flower preservatives also contain a respiration inhibitor which lowers the respiration rate of the flower. This is supposed to prevent burning of the flower's petals (the development of a brownish or blackish edge on the petal as the flower gets older) and thus increase flower life.

   Many people believe that an aspirin tablet in the water will improve the life of cut flowers. On this subject, the best advice is to take the aspirin yourself, but provide the flowers with fresh, room-temperature water. Best advice is to purchase from your florist one of the number of good quality flower preservatives on the market and use as directed. They are inexpensive, they work well, and they are worth far more than they cost.

3. *Cutting Carnation Stems*
It is best to cut carnation stems on a slant with a sharp knife. This provides maximum stem area for the absorption of water. It also prevents pinching of the vascular tissue in the stem which carries water up the stem. The cutting of carnation stems with a scissors tends to pinch the stem and can cause problems in the uptake of water needed by the flower head.

4. *Containers*
There are countless varieties of containers available. With low, flat bowls, it is difficult to provide enough water to cover stem areas. The provision of an adequate supply of water is, nonetheless, important. If the bowl is so flat that it will hold almost no water, then a small cup or other vessel should be placed in the center of the bowl where the flowers will be affixed in order to supply a reservoir for water.

The shape of bowls has an important influence on the shape of a flower arrangement and must always be considered by the floral designer in deciding what form or style of

arrangement he wants to make. Alabaster, marble or unglazed bowls which are porous can ruin furniture, carpeting or other areas on which they are placed, because water goes through them and collects where the bowl touches the surface. Generally speaking, this kind of container is unsatisfactory unless an impervious liner such as foil, plastic film or a small glass bowl is placed inside the container, or a nonporous saucer is put underneath the arrangement.

5. *Flower Holders*

A good flower arrangement is sturdy. The flowers and foliage are firmly held in place by a holder or a "frog" in which the flowers are affixed. Some of the holders which are commonly used are galvanized chicken wire, pin frogs, basket frogs, crushed styrofoam, and floral foam made specifically for this purpose. The frogs are placed inside the bowl and held in place by floral clay or tape. Floral foams are held in place by the confines of the bowl or taped in and also act as a water-holding material which helps to maintain an adequate supply of water for the flowers.

6. *Flower Arranging Tools*

Tools needed to make a flower arrangement are very simple – a sharp knife, some lengths of florist wire, florist or adhesive tape, floral clay, a flower holder of some sort (either

floral clay

chicken wire, pin frog or floral foam) and a pair of sharp scissors. The scissors should be used only to cut tape, ribbon, excessive foliage and other similar materials. They should not be used, as a rule, to cut the ends of flower stems.

7. *How to Make Carnations Last Longer*
Here are eight important do's and don'ts for making your carnation arrangements last longer:

a. Be sure the container has plenty of water available for the flowers and foliage at all times. Stick a finger in the bowl to check the water level and add water regularly, at least every other day. Use lukewarm water rather than very cold or very hot.

b. Use a floral preservative. Floral preservatives provide food – prevent fungus and algae growths and generally can be counted on to provide at least two to three extra days of flower life. Where floral preservatives are not used, it is necessary to recut the stems of the blooms in your arrangement and change the water completely every two or three days.

c. Use deep water where possible, as this provides hydraulic pressure to force the water up the stems.

d. Handle the flowers as little as possible when making your arrangement and after the arrangement is completed.
It is all right to move flowers in the bowl, but avoid picking them up and replacing them and touching the foliage or the petals as much as you can.

e. Keep the flowers out of warm or drafty places. Wind and heat increase plant respiration and speed the aging process.

f. As foliage and flowers die, remove them from the arrangement, adjust the remaining flowers to fill up the empty space, and you will increase the length of time your arrangement lasts.

g. Don't place carnations in arrangements containing fruits, particularly apples. Apples give off ethylene gas, and as little as two parts of ethylene gas per million parts of air will put carnations to sleep in a very short time.

h. Keep the flower-arranging bowls and frogs you use scrubbed and clean. A dirty bowl or frog containing the residue of a previous flower arrangement will develop algae and fungus growths more quickly and will usually shorten the life of a flower arrangement by several days. Scrub your bowls and frogs in a detergent mixture containing a little chlorine washing powder for the best results.